Praise for The Author

"As someone who knows the benefits of journaling, yet has never had the patience to sit down and write, I found Megan's guided journaling process to be incredibly intuitive and powerful. If you simply follow the prompts, you will find clarity around the issue(s) you wish to discern. Truly an amazing tool to help you access divine wisdom and ultimately peace."

    — Karla Heeter

"I entered into my first guided journaling experience hopeful and expectant, but not without some doubt. I have sometimes felt like I have a hard time hearing from God, and truly discerning his call for me or even the next best step. But, I was pleasantly surprised and inspired by the experience. The words flowed. At first I wasn't sure if they were my words or those of the Holy Spirit in me, but with Megan's assistance I found that Godly truths were indeed contained in the pages I filled and I left the experience with renewed clarity, faith, and connection to God the father!"

    — Tina Gilbreath

"The idea of listening for God's voice can seem daunting and through Megan's guidance, I was able to focus and gain clarity of his messages to me. Her process is one of peaceful observation which lends to transformational thinking for the participant."

    —Jill Seivert

"I thought my relationship with God was complete, but Beautiful Exchange Journaling changed my perspective. I could feel God closer to me than ever before. I learned He is my loving Father and He never changes. Megan helped me to know how to listen to God's voice and feel that peace that surpasses all understanding."

    — Marcela Macias

"Guided journaling, dialoguing the prompts of God in my heart, and recording that information as a reference for the future are invaluable to keep a record of the journey."

— **Marvin Harrell**

"I felt this journaling practice was a really sweet place to meet the Lord and to hear what God was saying to me. It gave me the confidence to say 'yes' to my next job and to go forward with joy."

— **Erin Reynolds**

"Beautiful exchange journaling is like a mini-date with the Holy Spirit!"

— **Colleen Cameron**

"I do not typically like to journal. So I was skeptical when Megan suggested I journal in order to hear from God. But her guided journaling really did help me focus on an issue I was struggling with and hear from God."

— **Leah Landolfi**

"I struggle to sit and journal on my own. I really enjoyed that Beautiful Exchange Journaling is guided step by step. This framework makes it less overwhelming for me and helps me focus on my heart and God's plan for me."

— **Janeen Hill**

"I have been a Christian my whole life. I was blessed to participate in a retreat with Megan learning how to journal and connect with God. I have always been intimidated by journaling! But after her retreat and using her helpful guidance on how to journal I am now much more confident and can truly see the benefit of it!"

— **Danielle Morrison**

"This journaling experience has been so important in my life. It has given me a written record of the joy, the pain - ultimately the raw material that the Lord is using to refine my perspective and set my understanding in a refreshed place."

— **Christina Harrell**

A Beautiful Exchange Journal

Untangled Faith

A Beautiful Exchange Journal

Untangled Faith

Megan B. Nilsen

For information on distribution rights, royalties, derivative works, or licensing opportunities on behalf of this content or work, please get in touch with the publisher at the address below:

Farmhouse Publishings, LLC,
P.O. Box 333
Spearfish, SD 57783

Holman Christian Standard Bible®, Holman CSB®, and HCSB® are federally registered trademarks of Holman Bible Publishers.

ESV® Text Edition: 2016. Copyright © 2001 by Crossway, a publishing ministry of Good News Publishers. The ESV® text has been reproduced in cooperation with and by permission of Good News Publishers. Unauthorized reproduction of this publication is prohibited.

ISBN: 978-1-7373708-7-1

Design by Heidi Caperton

Printed in the United States of America.

Your Beautiful Exchange

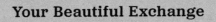

—

Month/Year   Month/Year

"If you truly desire intimacy with your Father and Jesus, you must be willing to do what is the very heart of intimacy: share who you really are with Him–all your innermost thoughts and feelings."

Linda Boone, Author[1]

"This is the word that came to Jeremiah from the LORD: 'This is what the LORD, the God of Israel says, 'Write in a book all the words I have spoken to you.'"

Jeremiah 30:1-2

"I will take my stand at my watch post and station myself on the tower, and look out to see what he will say to me, and what I will answer concerning my complaint. And the LORD answered me: 'Write the vision; make it plain on tablets, so he may run who reads it. For still the vision awaits its appointed time; it hastens to the end – it will not lie. If it seems slow, wait for it; it will surely come; it will not delay.'"

Habakkuk 2:1-3 ESV

"Write therefore the things that you have seen, those that are, and those that are to take place after this."

Revelation 1:19 ESV

1. *Journaling With God Quotes (2 quotes)*. (n.d.). https://www.goodreads.com/quotes/tag/journaling-with-god

Introduction

L ife is often complicated, stressful, broken, and messy. A good friend of mine plainly states, "Earth is hard."

While there are glorious seasons of mental clarity and great celebration, there are probably more occasions tangled in a web of challenging thoughts and emotions.

What are we to do in those hard places? To whom do we turn when we have more questions than answers?

If we want to untangle these overwhelming thoughts and move toward more profound connection, clarity, and peace, we must find ways to capture our thoughts and navigate the difficulty of life.

While King Solomon's words in Ecclesiastes 1:2 argue that "everything is futile," King David counters that when we shift our perspective and hope in the Lord, we will "have a future" and the ability to "keep [our] mind on the right course" (Proverbs 23:18-19).

The Apostle Paul reminds us, "we have not received the spirit of the world but the Spirit who comes from God, so that we may understand what has been freely given to us by God" (1 Corinthians 2:12).

What has been given to us?

As spiritual people, we can "evaluate everything" because "we have the mind of Christ" (1 Corinthians 2:15-16).

You have access to peace that is not of this world and supernatural counsel available to you through the power of the Holy Spirit. When you lean in and listen to the voice of God, you will receive wisdom and understanding. However, this practice is an art, not a science, and following Jesus is a relationship, not a formula.

While there are as many ways to hear from God as there are people on this earth, one thing, in particular, has helped me untangle my confounded thoughts and receive Kingdom perspective and revelation. This experiential approach enables me to pour out my heart and to question Jesus honestly, and then I humbly and intentionally listen as He responds with grace and truth.

To be clear, I did not make up the concept of journaling with God. In fact, I learned the art of two-way journaling from a wonderful teacher named Mark Virkler of *Commu-*

nion with God Ministries. I have been practicing it for a couple of years and find it useful to unlock deep-seated Kingdom wisdom with my life coaching clients.

One morning as I sat with the Lord, the Holy Spirit dropped a deeper concept of this journaling with a more profound writing framework and a series of layered, reflecting processes.

As I became aware of this, the detailed, all-encompassing blueprint—which goes beyond just releasing and receiving—came to my thoughts. That's when the multi-step "Beautiful Exchange Journaling" concept was born.

This journal provides a place to connect with Jesus and receive the good gifts and full life He promises. It is meant to impart His ways, correct confusion, and shepherd you into a life of spiritual wisdom and abundance. It encourages you to move toward every good work He prepared ahead of time for you to do (Ephesians 2:10).

This journal is a space where you can cry out to God on behalf of the people—a place where you can replace old, confused thoughts with new revelation and Kingdom perspective. To receive maximum benefit, try to quiet the ambient noise around you and center your heart and mind so you can be renewed in His presence today. Ask the Holy Spirit to come in and speak to you.

Throughout the pages of this journal, you can capture each moment, thought, question, or concern as they come and bring it to Jesus. He will use it to refine your perspective, renew your mind, and refresh your soul.

Beautiful Exchange journaling is a strategic, in-depth, intentional framework that expands on two-way journaling with added steps for reflection and activation. It helps to untangle any thoughts keeping you confused, frustrated, or stuck and move you into the love and goodness of God, the peace and truth of Jesus, and the wisdom and guidance of the Holy Spirit.

(If you want to dive deeper into hearing God's voice and understanding the foundational and biblical perspectives on each of these steps, please read the companion book I wrote titled **"Untangled Faith: How Honest Conversations with God Lead to Deeper Connections, Clarity, and Peace")**.

The following is a detailed explanation of each part of the daily journal exercise, step by step.

Before you start, get in touch with your body. How are you feeling? What emotion are you bringing to the practice? Write down a **"check in word"** to ground yourself in the present moment.

Take a deep breath and enter into the experience.

Step 1: Get Rooted in Scripture (Anchor). The first and most crucial step is to take a moment to shift your attention from the noise and distractions of the world, quiet your spirit, and anchor your soul in Scripture. I encourage you to read the selected passage several times to root yourself in His presence. Marinate in the Word and practice listening to God's voice.

Step 2: Record the Key Message (Notice). What feels important to you in those verses? Write down any word, phrase, or Kingdom truth that specifically stands out from the day's Scripture passage.

Step 3: Recognize God's Goodness (Gratitude). "Every good and perfect gift is from above, coming down from the Father of lights, who does not change like shifting shadows" (James 1:17). Therefore, in order to cultivate an awareness of God's goodness and present activity in your life, it is important to recognize the blessings. Once you are awake to His continuous presence, it's easier to access a fresh perspective on something that may not feel as much like a gift. Identify three things you are grateful for in your life right now.

Step 4: Release and Request (Pour Out). This section is wide open to pour your thoughts on the page. Ask any questions you have and bring them to Jesus! Share what weighs you down. Consider whatever is on your mind right now. Let your mind settle on something specific you want to flesh out with God.

What do you want to journal about today? Is there a particular decision you need to make? A stressful relationship that needs tending? Do you seek wisdom for your family, lifestyle, business, etc.? Anything goes. This is your chance to share whatever is on your mind as unfiltered communication from you to Jesus.

Before you begin - set a timer for four minutes. Why four minutes? If you're anything like me, you could fill pages and pages with your questions, complaints, and general confusion. An eternal gripe session is not what we're going for here. We want this to be a short but intense expression of your inner desires. Be completely honest. Don't censor yourself or hold anything back. Set the timer and let it rip. God can only redeem what you are willing to release. When the timer goes off, finish your thought and set down your pen.

Step 5: Receive Kingdom Perspective (Fill Up). You got your chance to get some things off your chest. Now it's time to shift your perspective, tune your ears, and hear from Jesus. Take a deep breath. Close your eyes for a few seconds to help you focus. Ask Jesus to speak to you and show you His perspective on your shared situation.

Write this section in the third person, as if Jesus speaks directly to you. This is His letter to you. Begin to write anything that comes to your mind. How does He address you? What does He call you? What words come into your mind? Again, don't think too hard or censor your thoughts.

Tune to the Holy Spirit flow and write whatever you hear. Feel free to draw what you see if you catch a vision instead of words. The point is not the medium. It's the message. Write until you are finished or the thoughts come to a close.

Step 6: Re-Read and Review (Pay Attention). Now look over the message you just received. Read what you wrote. What stands out to you as most important? What do you have questions about that may need further exploration? Highlight, circle, underline or star words or phrases that encapsulate the heart of the message. Then, list a couple of key points in this section. What practical truth have you received?

Step 7: Renew Your Mind (Find the Truth). What fundamental truth does God want you to know about His character, Kingdom, plans, and purposes for you and others? The Apostle Paul says true worship is for you to be "transformed by the renewing of your mind so that you may discern the good, pleasing, and perfect will of God" (Romans 12:2).

Step 8: Remove and Replace (Recognize - and Make - the Beautiful Exchange)! Name the gift of love Jesus offers you. What do you need to turn from, surrender, or let go of to walk in alignment with the Holy Spirit's truth and life?

> Fill in these blanks: I release _____ and replace it with_____.
> *(Remember, you are moving from flesh to Spirit - Romans 8:6).*

Step 9: Respond In Active Faith (Take Action). This is the "so what, now what" portion. Discern any Holy Spirit nudges or promptings and write down what action you feel led to take from here. What has the Counselor and Guide invited you to do (John 14:26)?

Step 10: Explore Any Resistance (Discern any Hesitation or Pushback). What feelings come up when you receive an invitation to walk in bold, active faith? As you go through this process, paying attention to your body's reaction is important. Do you feel your heart race? Do your palms sweat? Does your jaw clench? When my teeth grind and my neck muscles tense up, I know it's time to ask questions and pay attention to get to the root of what's really going on.

Step 11: Reach Out (Seek Confirmation). What counsel or confirmation do you need now? It's good and right to examine the word you received (1 Thessalonians 5:20-22). Is there a specific person you can talk to for health and accountability? Do you want to read more about this in Scripture? Make a plan for Godly counsel if needed (Proverbs 11:14).

Step 12: Reflect (Testify)! Look back over your journaling. As you reflect on the process, what would you like to say to Jesus in response to what He gave you? How do you feel now, and what's your commitment to God, yourself, and others moving forward (Psalm 77:12)?

After this, bring awareness back to your body and current emotion. How do you feel after this experience? Write your "check out" word in the final blank.

Wait, there's one last thing!

The most important details in this text are that if you follow Jesus, you are a child of God. As such, He can and will speak to you. If you are trying to connect with Jesus for the first time, the preliminary step is to show up open and expect to connect. Then, shut out the external (or internal) noise and lean in to listen to His still, small voice.

His voice will come, but you may wonder how to discern if you're receiving wisdom from heaven when so many thoughts flow through your head. How do you know if it's truly God's voice you hear?

James 3:17-18 provides an excellent framework to use when determining a message's source. As you review what you receive in your spirit, ask the following questions to confirm if Jesus is speaking. These evaluations will lead you toward deeper connection, clarity, and peace.

Is it pure? The first thing to consider is that wisdom from heaven will be apparent, clean, modest, and true. It is free from inappropriate elements or worldly suggestions.

Is it filled with peace? Does this word bring peaceful, loving solutions? Does it carry civility and harmony into your natural relationships? Does it calm your heart to hear this word?

Is it considerate and willing to yield to others? Is it gentle? Does it demonstrate a general awareness of other people's feelings? Does it submit to the authority of heaven? Is it full of mercy and good deeds? Does it lead you toward kindness and generosity? Will it help you bear the fruit of the Spirit? (i.e., love, joy, peace, patience, kindness, goodness, faithfulness, gentleness, and self-control).

Is it impartial and sincere? Do you have a personal agenda, or are you allowing the Holy Spirit to speak into your situation with an open heart? Ask the Lord to clear your mind of any obvious or hidden deceit.

If the answer to these questions is "yes," - then it stands to reason you are hearing from God!

In the **back of this journal**, you will notice a place to **log your "beautiful exchanges."** Each time you go through the entire exercise, you will have the chance to release something from your flesh and receive the gift of the Spirit. You can log the details as a record of testimony and chronicle your honest interactions with God. You will be able to see His good and gracious gifts materialize before your very eyes!

Now it's your turn!

Take a deep breath.

Settle your nerves.

And dive in!

Prepare to receive Kingdom wisdom, revelation, and guidance — one day, one step, one encounter at a time.

Journal

Today's Date

Check in word, how are you feeling right now?

_____   _____

Step 1: **Get Rooted in Scripture** (Anchor).

Take a moment to marinate in the following passage.

"Now this is what the LORD says– the one who created you, Jacob, and the
one who formed you, Israel – "Do not fear, for I have redeemed you; I have
called you by your name; you are mine. When you pass through the waters,
I will be with you, and the rivers will not overwhelm you. When you walk
through the fire, you will not be scorched, and the flame will not burn you."

— Isaiah 43:1-2

Step 2: **Record the Key Message** (Notice).

What Kingdom truth is God highlighting to you in this passage?

_____

_____

_____

_____

_____

Step 3: **Recognize God's Goodness** (Gratitude).

List three things you are grateful for today.

_____

_____

_____

_____

_____

Step 4: **Release and Request** (Pour Out).

Pour out your honest questions and concerns to the Lord.
What do you want to address with him?

Step 5: **Receive God's Perspective** (Fill Up).

Ask the Lord to fill your spirit with His words.

Write down what you hear Him say.

Step 6: **Re-Read and Review** (Pay Attention).
    What stands out to you?
    List key/highlighted parts of God's message to you.

_____

_____

_____

_____

_____

_____

Step 7: **Renew Your Mind** (Find the Truth).
    What specific truth does God want you to
    incorporate into your life today?

_____

_____

_____

_____

_____

_____

Step 8: **Remove and Replace** (Recognize - and Make - the Beautiful Exchange). What exchange does Jesus offer you?

Today I Release $\longrightarrow$

and replace it with $\longrightarrow$

Step 9: **Respond** (Take Action).

What step of faith do you sense God inviting you to take?

_____

_____

_____

Step 10: **Explore the Resistance** (Discern any Hesitation or Pushback).

What feelings come up for you when you receive an invitation to walk in bold, active faith? Where/how do you feel hesitation or pushback in your spirit?

_____

_____

_____

_____

Step 11: **Reach Out** (Seek Confirmation).

What counsel would help you to move forward?

_____

_____

_____

_____

Step 12: **Reflect** (Testify)!

What would you like to say to the Lord to close your journaling time? Write a word back to God in response to what you received today.

_____

_____

_____

_____

_____

_____

_____

_____

_____

_____

_____

_____

_____

_____

_____

_____

_____

_____

_____

_____

_____

_____

_____

_____

_____

Chronicle your beautiful exchange in the back of the book.

Today's Date

Check in word, how are you feeling right now?

_____   _____

Step 1: Get Rooted in Scripture (Anchor).

Take a moment to marinate in the following passage.

"See! I stand at the door and knock.
If anyone hears my voice and opens
the door, I will come in to him and
eat with him, and he with me."

— Revelation 3:20

Step 2: Record the Key Message (Notice).

What Kingdom truth is God highlighting to you in this passage?

_____

_____

_____

_____

_____

Step 3: Recognize God's Goodness (Gratitude).

List three things you are grateful for today.

_____

_____

_____

_____

_____

Step 4: **Release and Request** (Pour Out).

Pour out your honest questions and concerns to the Lord.
What do you want to address with him?

_____

_____

_____

_____

_____

_____

_____

_____

_____

_____

_____

_____

_____

_____

_____

_____

_____

_____

_____

_____

Step 5: **Receive God's Perspective** (Fill Up).

Ask the Lord to fill your spirit with His words.

Write down what you hear Him say.

Step 6: **Re-Read and Review** (Pay Attention).
What stands out to you?
List key/highlighted parts of God's message to you.

_____

_____

_____

_____

_____

_____

Step 7: **Renew Your Mind** (Find the Truth).
What specific truth does God want you to
incorporate into your life today?

_____

_____

_____

_____

_____

_____

Step 8: **Remove and Replace** (Recognize - and Make - the Beautiful
Exchange). What exchange does Jesus offer you?

Today I Release $\longrightarrow$

and replace it with $\longrightarrow$

Step 9: **Respond** (Take Action).

What step of faith do you sense God inviting you to take?

Step 10: **Explore the Resistance** (Discern any Hesitation or Pushback).

What feelings come up for you when you receive an invitation to walk in bold, active faith? Where/how do you feel hesitation or pushback in your spirit?

Step 11: **Reach Out** (Seek Confirmation).

What counsel would help you to move forward?

Step 12: **Reflect** (Testify)!

What would you like to say to the Lord to close your journaling time? Write a word back to God in response to what you received today.

Chronicle your beautiful exchange in the back of the book.

Today's Date

Check in word, how are you feeling right now?

_____

_____

Step 1: Get Rooted in Scripture (Anchor).

Take a moment to marinate in the following passage.

> "My sheep hear my voice, I know them,
> and they follow me. I give them eternal
> life, and they will never perish. No one
> will snatch them out of my hand."
>
> — **John 10:27-28**

Step 2: Record the Key Message (Notice).

What Kingdom truth is God highlighting to you in this passage?

_____

_____

_____

_____

_____

Step 3: Recognize God's Goodness (Gratitude).

List three things you are grateful for today.

_____

_____

_____

_____

_____

_____

Step 4: **Release and Request** (Pour Out).

Pour out your honest questions and concerns to the Lord. What do you want to address with him?

_____

_____

_____

_____

_____

_____

_____

_____

_____

_____

_____

_____

_____

_____

_____

_____

_____

_____

_____

Step 5: **Receive God's Perspective** (Fill Up).

Ask the Lord to fill your spirit with His words.

Write down what you hear Him say.

Step 6: **Re-Read and Review** (Pay Attention).
What stands out to you?
List key/highlighted parts of God's message to you.

_____

_____

_____

_____

_____

_____

_____

Step 7: **Renew Your Mind** (Find the Truth).
What specific truth does God want you to
incorporate into your life today?

_____

_____

_____

_____

_____

_____

_____

Step 8: **Remove and Replace** (Recognize - and Make - the Beautiful
Exchange). What exchange does Jesus offer you?

Today I Release ⟶

and replace it with ⟶

Step 9: **Respond** (Take Action).

What step of faith do you sense God inviting you to take?

_____

_____

_____

Step 10: **Explore the Resistance** (Discern any Hesitation or Pushback).

What feelings come up for you when you receive an invitation to walk in bold, active faith? Where/how do you feel hesitation or pushback in your spirit?

_____

_____

_____

Step 11: **Reach Out** (Seek Confirmation).

What counsel would help you to move forward?

_____

_____

_____

Step 12: **Reflect** (Testify)!

What would you like to say to the Lord to close your journaling time? Write a word back to God in response to what you received today.

_____

_____

_____

Chronicle your beautiful exchange in the back of the book.

Today's Date

Check in word, how are you feeling right now?

_____   _____

Step 1: Get Rooted in Scripture (Anchor).

Take a moment to marinate in the following passage.

"I will listen to what God will say;
surely the LORD will declare peace to
his people, his faithful ones, and not
let them go back to foolish ways."

— Psalm 85:8

Step 2: Record the Key Message (Notice).

What Kingdom truth is God highlighting to you in this passage?

_____

_____

_____

_____

_____

Step 3: Recognize God's Goodness (Gratitude).

List three things you are grateful for today.

_____

_____

_____

_____

_____

Step 4: **Release and Request** (Pour Out).

Pour out your honest questions and concerns to the Lord. What do you want to address with him?

Step 5: **Receive God's Perspective** (Fill Up).

Ask the Lord to fill your spirit with His words.

Write down what you hear Him say.

Step 6: **Re-Read and Review** (Pay Attention).
What stands out to you?
List key/highlighted parts of God's message to you.

_____

_____

_____

_____

_____

_____

Step 7: **Renew Your Mind** (Find the Truth).
What specific truth does God want you to
incorporate into your life today?

_____

_____

_____

_____

_____

_____

Step 8: **Remove and Replace** (Recognize - and Make - the Beautiful
Exchange). What exchange does Jesus offer you?

Today I Release $\longrightarrow$

and replace it with $\longrightarrow$

Step 9: **Respond** (Take Action).

What step of faith do you sense God inviting you to take?

_____

_____

_____

Step 10: **Explore the Resistance** (Discern any Hesitation or Pushback).

What feelings come up for you when you receive an invitation
to walk in bold, active faith? Where/how do you feel hesitation
or pushback in your spirit?

_____

_____

_____

Step 11: **Reach Out** (Seek Confirmation).

What counsel would help you to move forward?

_____

_____

_____

Step 12: **Reflect** (Testify)!

What would you like to say to the Lord to close your
journaling time? Write a word back to God in response
to what you received today.

_____

_____

_____

_____

_____

_____

_____

_____

_____

_____

_____

_____

_____

_____

_____

_____

_____

_____

_____

_____

_____

_____

_____

Chronicle your beautiful exchange in the back of the book.

Today's Date | Check in word, how are you feeling right now?

Step 1: **Get Rooted in Scripture** (Anchor).

Take a moment to marinate in the following passage.

"Carefully follow every command I
am giving you today, so that you may
live and increase, and may enter
and take possession of the land the
LORD swore to your ancestors."

— **Deuteronomy 8:1**

Step 2: **Record the Key Message** (Notice).

What Kingdom truth is God highlighting to you in this passage?

Step 3: **Recognize God's Goodness** (Gratitude).

List three things you are grateful for today.

Step 4: **Release and Request** (Pour Out).

      Pour out your honest questions and concerns to the Lord.
What do you want to address with him?

Step 5: **Receive God's Perspective** (Fill Up).

Ask the Lord to fill your spirit with His words.

Write down what you hear Him say.

Step 6: **Re-Read and Review** (Pay Attention).
What stands out to you?
List key/highlighted parts of God's message to you.

_____

_____

_____

_____

_____

_____

_____

Step 7: **Renew Your Mind** (Find the Truth).
What specific truth does God want you to
incorporate into your life today?

_____

_____

_____

_____

_____

_____

_____

Step 8: **Remove and Replace** (Recognize - and Make - the Beautiful
Exchange). What exchange does Jesus offer you?

Today I Release ⟶

and replace it with ⟶

Step 9: **Respond** (Take Action).
What step of faith do you sense God inviting you to take?

_____

_____

_____

Step 10: **Explore the Resistance** (Discern any Hesitation or Pushback).
What feelings come up for you when you receive an invitation
to walk in bold, active faith? Where/how do you feel hesitation
or pushback in your spirit?

_____

_____

_____

_____

Step 11: **Reach Out** (Seek Confirmation).
What counsel would help you to move forward?

_____

_____

_____

_____

Step 12: **Reflect** (Testify)!
What would you like to say to the Lord to close your
journaling time? Write a word back to God in response
to what you received today.

_____

_____

_____

_____

Chronicle your beautiful exchange in the back of the book.

Today's Date   Check in word, how are you feeling right now?

_____   _____

Step 1: **Get Rooted in Scripture** (Anchor).

Take a moment to marinate in the following passage.

> "For this is what love for God is: to keep his
> commands. And his commands are not a
> burden, because everyone who has been born
> of God conquers the world. This is the victory
> that has conquered the world: our faith."
>
> **— 1 John 5:3-4**

Step 2: **Record the Key Message** (Notice).

What Kingdom truth is God highlighting to you in this passage?

_____

_____

_____

_____

_____

Step 3: **Recognize God's Goodness** (Gratitude).

List three things you are grateful for today.

_____

_____

_____

_____

_____

Step 4: **Release and Request** (Pour Out).

Pour out your honest questions and concerns to the Lord. What do you want to address with him?

Step 5: **Receive God's Perspective** (Fill Up).

    Ask the Lord to fill your spirit with His words.

    Write down what you hear Him say.

_____

_____

_____

_____

_____

_____

_____

_____

_____

_____

_____

_____

_____

_____

_____

_____

_____

_____

_____

_____

_____

Step 6: **Re-Read and Review** (Pay Attention).
What stands out to you?
List key/highlighted parts of God's message to you.

_____

_____

_____

_____

_____

_____

Step 7: **Renew Your Mind** (Find the Truth).
What specific truth does God want you to
incorporate into your life today?

_____

_____

_____

_____

_____

_____

Step 8: **Remove and Replace** (Recognize - and Make - the Beautiful
Exchange). What exchange does Jesus offer you?

Today I Release $\longrightarrow$

and replace it with $\longrightarrow$

Step 9: **Respond** (Take Action).

What step of faith do you sense God inviting you to take?

_____

_____

_____

Step 10: **Explore the Resistance** (Discern any Hesitation or Pushback).

What feelings come up for you when you receive an invitation
to walk in bold, active faith? Where/how do you feel hesitation
or pushback in your spirit?

_____

_____

_____

Step 11: **Reach Out** (Seek Confirmation).

What counsel would help you to move forward?

_____

_____

_____

Step 12: **Reflect** (Testify)!

What would you like to say to the Lord to close your
journaling time? Write a word back to God in response
to what you received today.

_____

_____

_____

Chronicle your beautiful exchange in the back of the book.

Today's Date   Check in word, how are you feeling right now?

_____   _____

Step 1: Get Rooted in Scripture (Anchor).

> Take a moment to marinate in the following passage.

> "In the morning, LORD, you hear my
> voice; in the morning I plead my
> case to you and watch expectantly."
>
> **— Psalm 5:3**

Step 2: Record the Key Message (Notice).

> What Kingdom truth is God highlighting to you in this passage?

_____

_____

_____

_____

_____

Step 3: Recognize God's Goodness (Gratitude).

> List three things you are grateful for today.

_____

_____

_____

_____

_____

Step 4: **Release and Request** (Pour Out).

Pour out your honest questions and concerns to the Lord. What do you want to address with him?

Step 5: **Receive God's Perspective** (Fill Up).

    Ask the Lord to fill your spirit with His words.

    Write down what you hear Him say.

Step 6: **Re-Read and Review** (Pay Attention).

What stands out to you?

List key/highlighted parts of God's message to you.

Step 7: **Renew Your Mind** (Find the Truth).

What specific truth does God want you to incorporate into your life today?

Step 8: **Remove and Replace** (Recognize - and Make - the Beautiful Exchange). What exchange does Jesus offer you?

Today I Release ⟶

and replace it with ⟶

Step 9: **Respond** (Take Action).

What step of faith do you sense God inviting you to take?

_____

_____

_____

Step 10: **Explore the Resistance** (Discern any Hesitation or Pushback).

What feelings come up for you when you receive an invitation to walk in bold, active faith? Where/how do you feel hesitation or pushback in your spirit?

_____

_____

_____

Step 11: **Reach Out** (Seek Confirmation).

What counsel would help you to move forward?

_____

_____

_____

_____

Step 12: **Reflect** (Testify)!

What would you like to say to the Lord to close your journaling time? Write a word back to God in response to what you received today.

_____

_____

_____

_____

_____

_____

_____

_____

_____

_____

_____

_____

_____

_____

_____

_____

_____

_____

_____

_____

_____

_____

_____

Chronicle your beautiful exchange in the back of the book.

Today's Date   Check in word, how are you feeling right now?

_____   _____

Step 1: **Get Rooted in Scripture** (Anchor).

 Take a moment to marinate in the following passage.

> "The eyes of the LORD are on
> the righteous, and his ears are
> open to their cry for help."
>
> **— Psalm 34:15**

Step 2: **Record the Key Message** (Notice).

 What Kingdom truth is God highlighting to you in this passage?

_____

_____

_____

_____

_____

_____

Step 3: **Recognize God's Goodness** (Gratitude).

 List three things you are grateful for today.

_____

_____

_____

_____

_____

_____

Step 4: **Release and Request** (Pour Out).

Pour out your honest questions and concerns to the Lord.
What do you want to address with him?

Step 5: **Receive God's Perspective** (Fill Up).

Ask the Lord to fill your spirit with His words.

Write down what you hear Him say.

Step 6: **Re-Read and Review** (Pay Attention).
What stands out to you?
List key/highlighted parts of God's message to you.

Step 7: **Renew Your Mind** (Find the Truth).
What specific truth does God want you to
incorporate into your life today?

Step 8: **Remove and Replace** (Recognize - and Make - the Beautiful
Exchange). What exchange does Jesus offer you?

Today I Release $\longrightarrow$

and replace it with $\longrightarrow$

Step 9: **Respond** (Take Action).

What step of faith do you sense God inviting you to take?

_____

_____

_____

Step 10: **Explore the Resistance** (Discern any Hesitation or Pushback).

What feelings come up for you when you receive an invitation to walk in bold, active faith? Where/how do you feel hesitation or pushback in your spirit?

_____

_____

_____

Step 11: **Reach Out** (Seek Confirmation).

What counsel would help you to move forward?

_____

_____

_____

Step 12: **Reflect** (Testify)!

What would you like to say to the Lord to close your journaling time? Write a word back to God in response to what you received today.

_____

_____

_____

_____

Chronicle your beautiful exchange in the back of the book.

Today's Date   Check in word, how are you feeling right now?

_____   _____

Step 1: Get Rooted in Scripture (Anchor).

Take a moment to marinate in the following passage.

"The LORD who made the earth, the LORD
who forms it to establish it, the LORD
is his name, says this: Call to me and I
will answer you and tell you great and
incomprehensible things you do not know."

— Jeremiah 33:2-3

Step 2: Record the Key Message (Notice).

What Kingdom truth is God highlighting to you in this passage?

_____

_____

_____

_____

_____

Step 3: Recognize God's Goodness (Gratitude).

List three things you are grateful for today.

_____

_____

_____

_____

_____

Step 4: **Release and Request** (Pour Out).

Pour out your honest questions and concerns to the Lord. What do you want to address with him?

Step 5: **Receive God's Perspective** (Fill Up).

Ask the Lord to fill your spirit with His words.

Write down what you hear Him say.

Step 6: **Re-Read and Review** (Pay Attention).
What stands out to you?
List key/highlighted parts of God's message to you.

_____

_____

_____

_____

_____

_____

_____

Step 7: **Renew Your Mind** (Find the Truth).
What specific truth does God want you to
incorporate into your life today?

_____

_____

_____

_____

_____

_____

_____

Step 8: **Remove and Replace** (Recognize - and Make - the Beautiful
Exchange). What exchange does Jesus offer you?

Today I Release ⟶

and replace it with ⟶

Step 9: Respond (Take Action).

What step of faith do you sense God inviting you to take?

\
\

Step 10: Explore the Resistance (Discern any Hesitation or Pushback).

What feelings come up for you when you receive an invitation to walk in bold, active faith? Where/how do you feel hesitation or pushback in your spirit?

\
\

Step 11: Reach Out (Seek Confirmation).

What counsel would help you to move forward?

\
\

Step 12: Reflect (Testify)!

What would you like to say to the Lord to close your journaling time? Write a word back to God in response to what you received today.

Chronicle your beautiful exchange in the back of the book.

Today's Date   Check in word, how are you feeling right now?

_____   _____

Step 1: Get Rooted in Scripture (Anchor).

Take a moment to marinate in the following passage.

> "I waited patiently for the LORD, and he turned
> to me and heard my cry for help. He brought me
> up from a desolate pit, out of the muddy clay, and
> set my feet on a rock, making my steps secure."
>
> **— Psalm 40:1-2**

Step 2: Record the Key Message (Notice).

What Kingdom truth is God highlighting to you in this passage?

_____

_____

_____

_____

_____

Step 3: Recognize God's Goodness (Gratitude).

List three things you are grateful for today.

_____

_____

_____

_____

_____

Step 4: **Release and Request** (Pour Out).

    Pour out your honest questions and concerns to the Lord.

    What do you want to address with him?

Step 5: **Receive God's Perspective** (Fill Up).

Ask the Lord to fill your spirit with His words.

Write down what you hear Him say.

Step 6: **Re-Read and Review** (Pay Attention).
What stands out to you?
List key/highlighted parts of God's message to you.

Step 7: **Renew Your Mind** (Find the Truth).
What specific truth does God want you to
incorporate into your life today?

Step 8: **Remove and Replace** (Recognize - and Make - the Beautiful
Exchange). What exchange does Jesus offer you?

Today I Release ⟶

and replace it with ⟶

Step 9: **Respond** (Take Action).

What step of faith do you sense God inviting you to take?

_____

_____

_____

Step 10: **Explore the Resistance** (Discern any Hesitation or Pushback).

What feelings come up for you when you receive an invitation to walk in bold, active faith? Where/how do you feel hesitation or pushback in your spirit?

_____

_____

_____

_____

Step 11: **Reach Out** (Seek Confirmation).

What counsel would help you to move forward?

_____

_____

_____

_____

Step 12: **Reflect** (Testify)!

What would you like to say to the Lord to close your journaling time? Write a word back to God in response to what you received today.

_____

_____

_____

_____

_____

_____

_____

_____

_____

_____

_____

_____

_____

_____

_____

_____

_____

_____

_____

_____

_____

_____

_____

Chronicle your beautiful exchange in the back of the book.

Today's Date   Check in word, how are you feeling right now?

_____   _____

Step 1: Get Rooted in Scripture (Anchor).

Take a moment to marinate in the following passage.

"Above all, be strong and very courageous
to observe carefully the whole instruction
my servant Moses commanded you. Do not
turn from it to the right or the left, so that
you will have success wherever you go."

— Joshua 1:7

Step 2: Record the Key Message (Notice).

What Kingdom truth is God highlighting to you in this passage?

_____

_____

_____

_____

_____

Step 3: Recognize God's Goodness (Gratitude).

List three things you are grateful for today.

_____

_____

_____

_____

_____

_____

Step 4: **Release and Request** (Pour Out).

  Pour out your honest questions and concerns to the Lord.
  What do you want to address with him?

_____

_____

_____

_____

_____

_____

_____

_____

_____

_____

_____

_____

_____

_____

_____

_____

_____

_____

_____

_____

Step 5: **Receive God's Perspective** (Fill Up).

Ask the Lord to fill your spirit with His words.

Write down what you hear Him say.

Step 6: **Re-Read and Review** (Pay Attention).
What stands out to you?
List key/highlighted parts of God's message to you.

Step 7: **Renew Your Mind** (Find the Truth).
What specific truth does God want you to
incorporate into your life today?

Step 8: **Remove and Replace** (Recognize - and Make - the Beautiful
Exchange). What exchange does Jesus offer you?

Today I Release $\longrightarrow$

and replace it with $\longrightarrow$

Step 9: **Respond** (Take Action).

What step of faith do you sense God inviting you to take?

_____

_____

_____

Step 10: **Explore the Resistance** (Discern any Hesitation or Pushback).

What feelings come up for you when you receive an invitation to walk in bold, active faith? Where/how do you feel hesitation or pushback in your spirit?

_____

_____

_____

Step 11: **Reach Out** (Seek Confirmation).

What counsel would help you to move forward?

_____

_____

_____

Step 12: **Reflect** (Testify)!

What would you like to say to the Lord to close your journaling time? Write a word back to God in response to what you received today.

_____

_____

_____

_____

Chronicle your beautiful exchange in the back of the book.

Today's Date

Check in word, how are you feeling right now?

_____   _____

Step 1: Get Rooted in Scripture (Anchor).

Take a moment to marinate in the following passage.

"Sanctify them by the truth; your word is truth.
As you sent me into the world, I also have sent
them into the world. I sanctify myself for them, so
that they also may be sanctified by the truth."

— **John 17:17-19**

Step 2: Record the Key Message (Notice).

What Kingdom truth is God highlighting to you in this passage?

_____

_____

_____

_____

_____

_____

Step 3: Recognize God's Goodness (Gratitude).

List three things you are grateful for today.

_____

_____

_____

_____

_____

Step 4: **Release and Request** (Pour Out).

Pour out your honest questions and concerns to the Lord. What do you want to address with him?

_____

_____

_____

_____

_____

_____

_____

_____

_____

_____

_____

_____

_____

_____

_____

_____

_____

_____

_____

_____

Step 5: **Receive God's Perspective** (Fill Up).

Ask the Lord to fill your spirit with His words.

Write down what you hear Him say.

Step 6: **Re-Read and Review** (Pay Attention).
    What stands out to you?
    List key/highlighted parts of God's message to you.

_____

_____

_____

_____

_____

_____

_____

Step 7: **Renew Your Mind** (Find the Truth).
    What specific truth does God want you to
    incorporate into your life today?

_____

_____

_____

_____

_____

_____

_____

Step 8: **Remove and Replace** (Recognize - and Make - the Beautiful
Exchange). What exchange does Jesus offer you?

Today I Release ⟶

and replace it with ⟶

Step 9: **Respond** (Take Action).

What step of faith do you sense God inviting you to take?

_____

_____

_____

Step 10: **Explore the Resistance** (Discern any Hesitation or Pushback).

What feelings come up for you when you receive an invitation to walk in bold, active faith? Where/how do you feel hesitation or pushback in your spirit?

_____

_____

_____

Step 11: **Reach Out** (Seek Confirmation).

What counsel would help you to move forward?

_____

_____

_____

Step 12: **Reflect** (Testify)!

What would you like to say to the Lord to close your journaling time? Write a word back to God in response to what you received today.

_____

_____

_____

Chronicle your beautiful exchange in the back of the book.

Today's Date

Check in word, how are you feeling right now?

_____   _____

Step 1: **Get Rooted in Scripture** (Anchor).

Take a moment to marinate in the following passage.

"As for the seed that fell among thorns, these are the ones who, when they have heard, go on their way and are choked with worries, riches, and pleasures of life, and produce no mature fruit. But the seed in the good ground–these are the ones who, having heard the word with an honest and good heart, hold on to it and by enduring, produce fruit."

— **Luke 8:14-15**

Step 2: **Record the Key Message** (Notice).

What Kingdom truth is God highlighting to you in this passage?

_____

_____

_____

_____

_____

Step 3: **Recognize God's Goodness** (Gratitude).

List three things you are grateful for today.

_____

_____

_____

_____

_____

Step 4: **Release and Request** (Pour Out).

Pour out your honest questions and concerns to the Lord.
What do you want to address with him?

Step 5: **Receive God's Perspective** (Fill Up).

Ask the Lord to fill your spirit with His words.

Write down what you hear Him say.

Step 6: **Re-Read and Review** (Pay Attention).

      What stands out to you?

      List key/highlighted parts of God's message to you.

_____

_____

_____

_____

_____

_____

Step 7: **Renew Your Mind** (Find the Truth).

      What specific truth does God want you to
      incorporate into your life today?

_____

_____

_____

_____

_____

_____

Step 8: **Remove and Replace** (Recognize - and Make - the Beautiful Exchange). What exchange does Jesus offer you?

      Today I Release $\longrightarrow$

      and replace it with $\longrightarrow$

Step 9: **Respond** (Take Action).

      What step of faith do you sense God inviting you to take?

Step 10: **Explore the Resistance** (Discern any Hesitation or Pushback).

      What feelings come up for you when you receive an invitation to walk in bold, active faith? Where/how do you feel hesitation or pushback in your spirit?

Step 11: **Reach Out** (Seek Confirmation).

      What counsel would help you to move forward?

Step 12: **Reflect** (Testify)!

      What would you like to say to the Lord to close your journaling time? Write a word back to God in response to what you received today.

Chronicle your beautiful exchange in the back of the book.

Today's Date   Check in word, how are you feeling right now?

_____   _____

Step 1: Get Rooted in Scripture (Anchor).

    Take a moment to marinate in the following passage.

> "I have told you these things so that in
> me you may have peace. You will have
> suffering in this world. Be courageous!
> I have conquered the world."
>
> **— John 16:33**

Step 2: Record the Key Message (Notice).

    What Kingdom truth is God highlighting to you in this passage?

_____

_____

_____

_____

_____

Step 3: Recognize God's Goodness (Gratitude).

    List three things you are grateful for today.

_____

_____

_____

_____

_____

Step 4: **Release and Request** (Pour Out).

Pour out your honest questions and concerns to the Lord.
What do you want to address with him?

_____

_____

_____

_____

_____

_____

_____

_____

_____

_____

_____

_____

_____

_____

_____

_____

_____

_____

_____

Step 5: **Receive God's Perspective** (Fill Up).

Ask the Lord to fill your spirit with His words.

Write down what you hear Him say.

Step 6: **Re-Read and Review** (Pay Attention).
  What stands out to you?
  List key/highlighted parts of God's message to you.

Step 7: **Renew Your Mind** (Find the Truth).
  What specific truth does God want you to
  incorporate into your life today?

Step 8: **Remove and Replace** (Recognize - and Make - the Beautiful
Exchange). What exchange does Jesus offer you?

  Today I Release $\longrightarrow$

  and replace it with $\longrightarrow$

Step 9: **Respond** (Take Action).

What step of faith do you sense God inviting you to take?

_____

_____

_____

Step 10: **Explore the Resistance** (Discern any Hesitation or Pushback).

What feelings come up for you when you receive an invitation to walk in bold, active faith? Where/how do you feel hesitation or pushback in your spirit?

_____

_____

_____

_____

Step 11: **Reach Out** (Seek Confirmation).

What counsel would help you to move forward?

_____

_____

_____

_____

Step 12: **Reflect** (Testify)!

What would you like to say to the Lord to close your journaling time? Write a word back to God in response to what you received today.

_____

_____

_____

_____

Chronicle your beautiful exchange in the back of the book.

Today's Date   Check in word, how are you feeling right now?

Step 1: **Get Rooted in Scripture** (Anchor).

Take a moment to marinate in the following passage.

"'For nothing will be impossible with
God.' 'See, I am the Lord's servant,' said
Mary. 'May it happen to me as you
have said.' Then the angel left her."

— Luke 1:37-38

Step 2: **Record the Key Message** (Notice).

What Kingdom truth is God highlighting to you in this passage?

Step 3: **Recognize God's Goodness** (Gratitude).

List three things you are grateful for today.

Step 4: **Release and Request** (Pour Out).

Pour out your honest questions and concerns to the Lord.
What do you want to address with him?

_____

_____

_____

_____

_____

_____

_____

_____

_____

_____

_____

_____

_____

_____

_____

_____

_____

_____

_____

_____

_____

Step 5: **Receive God's Perspective** (Fill Up).

Ask the Lord to fill your spirit with His words.

Write down what you hear Him say.

Step 6: **Re-Read and Review** (Pay Attention).
   What stands out to you?
   List key/highlighted parts of God's message to you.

Step 7: **Renew Your Mind** (Find the Truth).
   What specific truth does God want you to
   incorporate into your life today?

Step 8: **Remove and Replace** (Recognize - and Make - the Beautiful
Exchange). What exchange does Jesus offer you?

   Today I Release $\longrightarrow$

   and replace it with $\longrightarrow$

Step 9: **Respond** (Take Action).

What step of faith do you sense God inviting you to take?

Step 10: **Explore the Resistance** (Discern any Hesitation or Pushback).

What feelings come up for you when you receive an invitation to walk in bold, active faith? Where/how do you feel hesitation or pushback in your spirit?

Step 11: **Reach Out** (Seek Confirmation).

What counsel would help you to move forward?

Step 12: **Reflect** (Testify)!

What would you like to say to the Lord to close your journaling time? Write a word back to God in response to what you received today.

Chronicle your beautiful exchange in the back of the book.

Today's Date   Check in word, how are you feeling right now?

_____   _____

Step 1: **Get Rooted in Scripture** (Anchor).

Take a moment to marinate in the following passage.

> "Now if any of you lacks wisdom, he should ask
> God–who gives to all generously and ungrudgingly–
> and it will be given to him. But let him ask in
> faith without doubting. For the doubter is like the
> surging sea, driven and tossed by the wind."
>
> **— James 1:5-6**

Step 2: **Record the Key Message** (Notice).

What Kingdom truth is God highlighting to you in this passage?

_____

_____

_____

_____

_____

Step 3: **Recognize God's Goodness** (Gratitude).

List three things you are grateful for today.

_____

_____

_____

_____

_____

Step 4: **Release and Request** (Pour Out).

   Pour out your honest questions and concerns to the Lord.
   What do you want to address with him?

Step 5: **Receive God's Perspective** (Fill Up).

   Ask the Lord to fill your spirit with His words.

   Write down what you hear Him say.

Step 6: **Re-Read and Review** (Pay Attention).
What stands out to you?
List key/highlighted parts of God's message to you.

_____

_____

_____

_____

_____

_____

_____

Step 7: **Renew Your Mind** (Find the Truth).
What specific truth does God want you to
incorporate into your life today?

_____

_____

_____

_____

_____

_____

_____

Step 8: **Remove and Replace** (Recognize - and Make - the Beautiful
Exchange). What exchange does Jesus offer you?

Today I Release $\longrightarrow$

and replace it with $\longrightarrow$

Step 9: **Respond** (Take Action).

What step of faith do you sense God inviting you to take?

Step 10: **Explore the Resistance** (Discern any Hesitation or Pushback).

What feelings come up for you when you receive an invitation to walk in bold, active faith? Where/how do you feel hesitation or pushback in your spirit?

Step 11: **Reach Out** (Seek Confirmation).

What counsel would help you to move forward?

Step 12: **Reflect** (Testify)!

What would you like to say to the Lord to close your journaling time? Write a word back to God in response to what you received today.

Chronicle your beautiful exchange in the back of the book.

Today's Date   Check in word, how are you feeling right now?

_____   _____

Step 1: **Get Rooted in Scripture** (Anchor).

    Take a moment to marinate in the following passage.

> "'For my thoughts are not your thoughts, and
> your ways are not my ways.' This is the LORD's
> declaration. 'For as heaven is higher than
> earth, so my ways are higher than your ways,
> and my thoughts than your thoughts. '"
>
> **— Isaiah 55:8-9**

Step 2: **Record the Key Message** (Notice).

    What Kingdom truth is God highlighting to you in this passage?

_____

_____

_____

_____

_____

Step 3: **Recognize God's Goodness** (Gratitude).

    List three things you are grateful for today.

_____

_____

_____

_____

_____

Step 4: Release and Request (Pour Out).

Pour out your honest questions and concerns to the Lord.
What do you want to address with him?

_____

_____

_____

_____

_____

_____

_____

_____

_____

_____

_____

_____

_____

_____

_____

_____

_____

_____

_____

_____

_____

_____

_____

Step 5: **Receive God's Perspective** (Fill Up).

Ask the Lord to fill your spirit with His words.
Write down what you hear Him say.

Step 6: **Re-Read and Review** (Pay Attention).
　　　　What stands out to you?
　　　　List key/highlighted parts of God's message to you.

_____

_____

_____

_____

_____

_____

_____

Step 7: **Renew Your Mind** (Find the Truth).
　　　　What specific truth does God want you to
　　　　incorporate into your life today?

_____

_____

_____

_____

_____

_____

_____

Step 8: **Remove and Replace** (Recognize - and Make - the Beautiful
Exchange). What exchange does Jesus offer you?

　　　　　　Today I Release ⟶

　　　　　　and replace it with ⟶

Step 9: **Respond** (Take Action).

What step of faith do you sense God inviting you to take?

_____

_____

_____

Step 10: **Explore the Resistance** (Discern any Hesitation or Pushback).

What feelings come up for you when you receive an invitation to walk in bold, active faith? Where/how do you feel hesitation or pushback in your spirit?

_____

_____

_____

_____

Step 11: **Reach Out** (Seek Confirmation).

What counsel would help you to move forward?

_____

_____

_____

_____

Step 12: **Reflect** (Testify)!

What would you like to say to the Lord to close your journaling time? Write a word back to God in response to what you received today.

_____

_____

_____

_____

Chronicle your beautiful exchange in the back of the book.

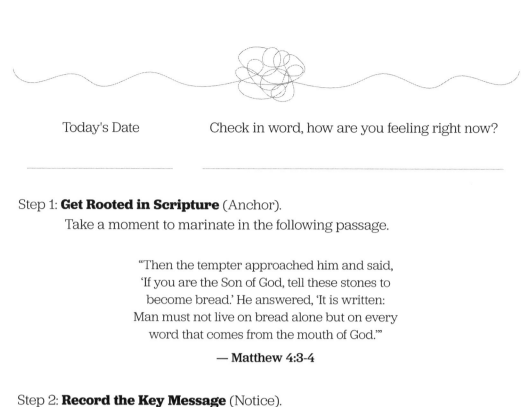

Today's Date   Check in word, how are you feeling right now?

_____   _____

Step 1: **Get Rooted in Scripture** (Anchor).

Take a moment to marinate in the following passage.

"Then the tempter approached him and said,
'If you are the Son of God, tell these stones to
become bread.' He answered, 'It is written:
Man must not live on bread alone but on every
word that comes from the mouth of God.'"

— **Matthew 4:3-4**

Step 2: **Record the Key Message** (Notice).

What Kingdom truth is God highlighting to you in this passage?

_____

_____

_____

_____

_____

Step 3: **Recognize God's Goodness** (Gratitude).

List three things you are grateful for today.

_____

_____

_____

_____

_____

_____

Step 4: Release and Request (Pour Out).

Pour out your honest questions and concerns to the Lord.
What do you want to address with him?

Step 5: **Receive God's Perspective** (Fill Up).

Ask the Lord to fill your spirit with His words.

Write down what you hear Him say.

Step 6: **Re-Read and Review** (Pay Attention).
      What stands out to you?
      List key/highlighted parts of God's message to you.

_____

_____

_____

_____

_____

_____

_____

Step 7: **Renew Your Mind** (Find the Truth).
      What specific truth does God want you to
      incorporate into your life today?

_____

_____

_____

_____

_____

_____

Step 8: **Remove and Replace** (Recognize - and Make - the Beautiful Exchange). What exchange does Jesus offer you?

        Today I Release $\longrightarrow$

        and replace it with $\longrightarrow$

Step 9: **Respond** (Take Action).

What step of faith do you sense God inviting you to take?

_____

_____

_____

Step 10: **Explore the Resistance** (Discern any Hesitation or Pushback).

What feelings come up for you when you receive an invitation to walk in bold, active faith? Where/how do you feel hesitation or pushback in your spirit?

_____

_____

_____

Step 11: **Reach Out** (Seek Confirmation).

What counsel would help you to move forward?

_____

_____

_____

Step 12: **Reflect** (Testify)!

What would you like to say to the Lord to close your journaling time? Write a word back to God in response to what you received today.

_____

_____

_____

Chronicle your beautiful exchange in the back of the book.

Today's Date

Check in word, how are you feeling right now?

_____   _____

Step 1: Get Rooted in Scripture (Anchor).

Take a moment to marinate in the following passage.

"For the LORD gives wisdom; from his mouth
come knowledge and understanding.He stores up
success for the upright; He is a shield for those who
live with integrity so that he may guard the paths of
justice and protect the way of his faithful followers."

— Proverbs 2:6-8

Step 2: Record the Key Message (Notice).

What Kingdom truth is God highlighting to you in this passage?

_____

_____

_____

_____

_____

Step 3: Recognize God's Goodness (Gratitude).

List three things you are grateful for today.

_____

_____

_____

_____

_____

_____

Step 4: **Release and Request** (Pour Out).
    Pour out your honest questions and concerns to the Lord.
    What do you want to address with him?

Step 5: **Receive God's Perspective** (Fill Up).

Ask the Lord to fill your spirit with His words.

Write down what you hear Him say.

Step 6: **Re-Read and Review** (Pay Attention).
    What stands out to you?
    List key/highlighted parts of God's message to you.

Step 7: **Renew Your Mind** (Find the Truth).
    What specific truth does God want you to
    incorporate into your life today?

Step 8: **Remove and Replace** (Recognize - and Make - the Beautiful
Exchange). What exchange does Jesus offer you?

Today I Release $\longrightarrow$

and replace it with $\longrightarrow$

Step 9: **Respond** (Take Action).

What step of faith do you sense God inviting you to take?

_____

_____

_____

Step 10: **Explore the Resistance** (Discern any Hesitation or Pushback).

What feelings come up for you when you receive an invitation
to walk in bold, active faith? Where/how do you feel hesitation
or pushback in your spirit?

_____

_____

_____

Step 11: **Reach Out** (Seek Confirmation).

What counsel would help you to move forward?

_____

_____

_____

Step 12: **Reflect** (Testify)!

What would you like to say to the Lord to close your
journaling time? Write a word back to God in response
to what you received today.

_____

_____

_____

_____

Chronicle your beautiful exchange in the back of the book.

Today's Date   Check in word, how are you feeling right now?

_____   _____

Step 1: **Get Rooted in Scripture** (Anchor).

Take a moment to marinate in the following passage.

"Trust in the LORD with all your heart, and
do not rely on your own understanding;
in all your ways know him, and he
will make your paths straight."

— Proverbs 3:5-6

Step 2: **Record the Key Message** (Notice).

What Kingdom truth is God highlighting to you in this passage?

_____

_____

_____

_____

_____

_____

Step 3: **Recognize God's Goodness** (Gratitude).

List three things you are grateful for today.

_____

_____

_____

_____

_____

_____

Step 4: **Release and Request** (Pour Out).

> Pour out your honest questions and concerns to the Lord.
> What do you want to address with him?

_____

_____

_____

_____

_____

_____

_____

_____

_____

_____

_____

_____

_____

_____

_____

_____

_____

_____

_____

Step 5: **Receive God's Perspective** (Fill Up).

Ask the Lord to fill your spirit with His words.

Write down what you hear Him say.

Step 6: **Re-Read and Review** (Pay Attention).
      What stands out to you?
      List key/highlighted parts of God's message to you.

Step 7: **Renew Your Mind** (Find the Truth).
      What specific truth does God want you to
      incorporate into your life today?

Step 8: **Remove and Replace** (Recognize - and Make - the Beautiful Exchange). What exchange does Jesus offer you?

Today I Release ⟶

and replace it with ⟶

Step 9: **Respond** (Take Action).

What step of faith do you sense God inviting you to take?

Step 10: **Explore the Resistance** (Discern any Hesitation or Pushback).

What feelings come up for you when you receive an invitation to walk in bold, active faith? Where/how do you feel hesitation or pushback in your spirit?

Step 11: **Reach Out** (Seek Confirmation).

What counsel would help you to move forward?

Step 12: **Reflect** (Testify)!

What would you like to say to the Lord to close your journaling time? Write a word back to God in response to what you received today.

Chronicle your beautiful exchange in the back of the book.

Today's Date   Check in word, how are you feeling right now?

....

Step 1: Get Rooted in Scripture (Anchor).

Take a moment to marinate in the following passage.

"Ask, and it will be given to you. Seek, and you
will find. Knock, and the door will be opened
to you. For everyone who asks receives,
and the one who seeks finds, and to the one
who knocks, the door will be opened."

— Matthew 7:7-8

Step 2: Record the Key Message (Notice).

What Kingdom truth is God highlighting to you in this passage?

_____

_____

_____

_____

_____

Step 3: Recognize God's Goodness (Gratitude).

List three things you are grateful for today.

_____

_____

_____

_____

_____

Step 4: **Release and Request** (Pour Out).

 Pour out your honest questions and concerns to the Lord.
 What do you want to address with him?

_____

_____

_____

_____

_____

_____

_____

_____

_____

_____

_____

_____

_____

_____

_____

_____

_____

_____

_____

Step 5: **Receive God's Perspective** (Fill Up).

Ask the Lord to fill your spirit with His words.

Write down what you hear Him say.

Step 6: **Re-Read and Review** (Pay Attention).

What stands out to you?

List key/highlighted parts of God's message to you.

_____

_____

_____

_____

_____

_____

_____

Step 7: **Renew Your Mind** (Find the Truth).

What specific truth does God want you to incorporate into your life today?

_____

_____

_____

_____

_____

_____

_____

Step 8: **Remove and Replace** (Recognize - and Make - the Beautiful Exchange). What exchange does Jesus offer you?

Today I Release ⟶

and replace it with ⟶

Step 9: **Respond** (Take Action).

What step of faith do you sense God inviting you to take?

Step 10: **Explore the Resistance** (Discern any Hesitation or Pushback).

What feelings come up for you when you receive an invitation to walk in bold, active faith? Where/how do you feel hesitation or pushback in your spirit?

Step 11: **Reach Out** (Seek Confirmation).

What counsel would help you to move forward?

Step 12: **Reflect** (Testify)!

What would you like to say to the Lord to close your journaling time? Write a word back to God in response to what you received today.

Chronicle your beautiful exchange in the back of the book.

Today's Date   Check in word, how are you feeling right now?

_____   _____

Step 1: Get Rooted in Scripture (Anchor).

Take a moment to marinate in the following passage.

> "Therefore, everyone who hears these words of mine
> and acts on them will be like a wise man who built his
> house on the rock. The rain fell, the rivers rose, and
> the winds blew and pounded that house. Yet it didn't
> collapse, because its foundation was on the rock."
>
> **— Matthew 7:24-25**

Step 2: Record the Key Message (Notice).

What Kingdom truth is God highlighting to you in this passage?

_____

_____

_____

_____

_____

Step 3: Recognize God's Goodness (Gratitude).

List three things you are grateful for today.

_____

_____

_____

_____

_____

Step 4: **Release and Request** (Pour Out).

Pour out your honest questions and concerns to the Lord.
What do you want to address with him?

Step 5: **Receive God's Perspective** (Fill Up).

Ask the Lord to fill your spirit with His words.

Write down what you hear Him say.

Step 6: **Re-Read and Review** (Pay Attention).
What stands out to you?
List key/highlighted parts of God's message to you.

_____

_____

_____

_____

_____

_____

_____

Step 7: **Renew Your Mind** (Find the Truth).
What specific truth does God want you to
incorporate into your life today?

_____

_____

_____

_____

_____

_____

_____

Step 8: **Remove and Replace** (Recognize - and Make - the Beautiful
Exchange). What exchange does Jesus offer you?

Today I Release ⟶

and replace it with ⟶

Step 9: **Respond** (Take Action).

What step of faith do you sense God inviting you to take?

_____

_____

_____

Step 10: **Explore the Resistance** (Discern any Hesitation or Pushback).

What feelings come up for you when you receive an invitation to walk in bold, active faith? Where/how do you feel hesitation or pushback in your spirit?

_____

_____

_____

_____

Step 11: **Reach Out** (Seek Confirmation).

What counsel would help you to move forward?

_____

_____

_____

Step 12: **Reflect** (Testify)!

What would you like to say to the Lord to close your journaling time? Write a word back to God in response to what you received today.

_____

_____

_____

_____

Chronicle your beautiful exchange in the back of the book.

Today's Date   Check in word, how are you feeling right now?

_____   _____

Step 1: Get Rooted in Scripture (Anchor).

Take a moment to marinate in the following passage.

> "I have spoken these things to you while
> I remain with you. But the Counselor, the
> Holy Spirit, whom the Father will send in my
> name, will teach you all things and remind
> you of everything I have told you."
>
> **— John 14:25-26**

Step 2: Record the Key Message (Notice).

What Kingdom truth is God highlighting to you in this passage?

_____

_____

_____

_____

_____

Step 3: Recognize God's Goodness (Gratitude).

List three things you are grateful for today.

_____

_____

_____

_____

_____

Step 4: **Release and Request** (Pour Out).

Pour out your honest questions and concerns to the Lord.
What do you want to address with him?

_____

_____

_____

_____

_____

_____

_____

_____

_____

_____

_____

_____

_____

_____

_____

_____

_____

_____

_____

_____

_____

_____

Step 5: **Receive God's Perspective** (Fill Up).

Ask the Lord to fill your spirit with His words.

Write down what you hear Him say.

Step 6: **Re-Read and Review** (Pay Attention).

What stands out to you?

List key/highlighted parts of God's message to you.

_____

_____

_____

_____

_____

_____

_____

Step 7: **Renew Your Mind** (Find the Truth).

What specific truth does God want you to
incorporate into your life today?

_____

_____

_____

_____

_____

_____

_____

Step 8: **Remove and Replace** (Recognize - and Make - the Beautiful
Exchange). What exchange does Jesus offer you?

Today I Release ⟶

and replace it with ⟶

Step 9: **Respond** (Take Action).

What step of faith do you sense God inviting you to take?

_____

_____

Step 10: **Explore the Resistance** (Discern any Hesitation or Pushback).

What feelings come up for you when you receive an invitation
to walk in bold, active faith? Where/how do you feel hesitation
or pushback in your spirit?

_____

_____

_____

Step 11: **Reach Out** (Seek Confirmation).

What counsel would help you to move forward?

_____

_____

_____

Step 12: **Reflect** (Testify)!

What would you like to say to the Lord to close your
journaling time? Write a word back to God in response
to what you received today.

_____

_____

_____

Chronicle your beautiful exchange in the back of the book.

Today's Date   Check in word, how are you feeling right now?

....

Step 1: Get Rooted in Scripture (Anchor).

Take a moment to marinate in the following passage.

"I rejoice in the way revealed by your
decrees as much as in all riches.
I will meditate on your precepts
and think about your ways."

— **Psalm 119:14-15**

Step 2: Record the Key Message (Notice).

What Kingdom truth is God highlighting to you in this passage?

....

....

....

....

....

Step 3: Recognize God's Goodness (Gratitude).

List three things you are grateful for today.

....

....

....

....

....

Step 4: **Release and Request** (Pour Out).

    Pour out your honest questions and concerns to the Lord.

    What do you want to address with him?

Step 5: **Receive God's Perspective** (Fill Up).

    Ask the Lord to fill your spirit with His words.

    Write down what you hear Him say.

Step 6: **Re-Read and Review** (Pay Attention).
What stands out to you?
List key/highlighted parts of God's message to you.

_____

_____

_____

_____

_____

_____

_____

Step 7: **Renew Your Mind** (Find the Truth).
What specific truth does God want you to
incorporate into your life today?

_____

_____

_____

_____

_____

_____

_____

Step 8: **Remove and Replace** (Recognize - and Make - the Beautiful
Exchange). What exchange does Jesus offer you?

Today I Release ⟶

and replace it with ⟶

Step 9: **Respond** (Take Action).

What step of faith do you sense God inviting you to take?

_____

_____

_____

Step 10: **Explore the Resistance** (Discern any Hesitation or Pushback).

What feelings come up for you when you receive an invitation to walk in bold, active faith? Where/how do you feel hesitation or pushback in your spirit?

_____

_____

_____

_____

Step 11: **Reach Out** (Seek Confirmation).

What counsel would help you to move forward?

_____

_____

_____

_____

Step 12: **Reflect** (Testify)!

What would you like to say to the Lord to close your journaling time? Write a word back to God in response to what you received today.

_____

_____

_____

_____

Chronicle your beautiful exchange in the back of the book.

Today's Date   Check in word, how are you feeling right now?

_____   _____

Step 1: Get Rooted in Scripture (Anchor).

Take a moment to marinate in the following passage.

"When the Spirit of truth comes, he
will guide you into all the truth. For
he will not speak on his own, but he
will speak whatever he hears. He will
also declare to you what is to come."

— **John 16:13**

Step 2: Record the Key Message (Notice).

What Kingdom truth is God highlighting to you in this passage?

_____

_____

_____

_____

_____

Step 3: Recognize God's Goodness (Gratitude).

List three things you are grateful for today.

_____

_____

_____

_____

_____

Step 4: **Release and Request** (Pour Out).

    Pour out your honest questions and concerns to the Lord.
What do you want to address with him?

_____

_____

_____

_____

_____

_____

_____

_____

_____

_____

_____

_____

_____

_____

_____

_____

_____

_____

_____

_____

Step 5: **Receive God's Perspective** (Fill Up).

Ask the Lord to fill your spirit with His words.

Write down what you hear Him say.

Step 6: **Re-Read and Review** (Pay Attention).
What stands out to you?
List key/highlighted parts of God's message to you.

_____

_____

_____

_____

_____

_____

_____

Step 7: **Renew Your Mind** (Find the Truth).
What specific truth does God want you to
incorporate into your life today?

_____

_____

_____

_____

_____

_____

_____

Step 8: **Remove and Replace** (Recognize - and Make - the Beautiful
Exchange). What exchange does Jesus offer you?

Today I Release ⟶

and replace it with ⟶

Step 9: **Respond** (Take Action).
What step of faith do you sense God inviting you to take?

Step 10: **Explore the Resistance** (Discern any Hesitation or Pushback).
What feelings come up for you when you receive an invitation to walk in bold, active faith? Where/how do you feel hesitation or pushback in your spirit?

Step 11: **Reach Out** (Seek Confirmation).
What counsel would help you to move forward?

Step 12: **Reflect** (Testify)!
What would you like to say to the Lord to close your journaling time? Write a word back to God in response to what you received today.

Chronicle your beautiful exchange in the back of the book.

Today's Date   Check in word, how are you feeling right now?

_____   _____

Step 1: Get Rooted in Scripture (Anchor).

    Take a moment to marinate in the following passage.

> "For this reason, we must pay attention
> all the more to what we have heard,
> so that we will not drift away."
>
> **— Hebrews 2:1**

Step 2: Record the Key Message (Notice).

    What Kingdom truth is God highlighting to you in this passage?

_____

_____

_____

_____

_____

_____

Step 3: Recognize God's Goodness (Gratitude).

    List three things you are grateful for today.

_____

_____

_____

_____

_____

_____

Step 4: **Release and Request** (Pour Out).

    Pour out your honest questions and concerns to the Lord.
What do you want to address with him?

Step 5: **Receive God's Perspective** (Fill Up).

Ask the Lord to fill your spirit with His words.

Write down what you hear Him say.

Step 6: **Re-Read and Review** (Pay Attention).
What stands out to you?
List key/highlighted parts of God's message to you.

_____

_____

_____

_____

_____

_____

_____

Step 7: **Renew Your Mind** (Find the Truth).
What specific truth does God want you to
incorporate into your life today?

_____

_____

_____

_____

_____

_____

_____

Step 8: **Remove and Replace** (Recognize - and Make - the Beautiful
Exchange). What exchange does Jesus offer you?

Today I Release ⟶

and replace it with ⟶

Step 9: **Respond** (Take Action).

What step of faith do you sense God inviting you to take?

_____

_____

_____

Step 10: **Explore the Resistance** (Discern any Hesitation or Pushback).

What feelings come up for you when you receive an invitation to walk in bold, active faith? Where/how do you feel hesitation or pushback in your spirit?

_____

_____

_____

_____

Step 11: **Reach Out** (Seek Confirmation).

What counsel would help you to move forward?

_____

_____

_____

_____

Step 12: **Reflect** (Testify)!

What would you like to say to the Lord to close your journaling time? Write a word back to God in response to what you received today.

_____

_____

_____

_____

Chronicle your beautiful exchange in the back of the book.

Today's Date   Check in word, how are you feeling right now?

_____   _____

Step 1: Get Rooted in Scripture (Anchor).

Take a moment to marinate in the following passage.

> "So faith comes from what is heard,
> and what is heard comes through
> the message about Christ."
>
> **— Romans 10:17**

Step 2: Record the Key Message (Notice).

What Kingdom truth is God highlighting to you in this passage?

_____

_____

_____

_____

_____

Step 3: Recognize God's Goodness (Gratitude).

List three things you are grateful for today.

_____

_____

_____

_____

_____

_____

Step 4: **Release and Request** (Pour Out).

Pour out your honest questions and concerns to the Lord.
What do you want to address with him?

_____

_____

_____

_____

_____

_____

_____

_____

_____

_____

_____

_____

_____

_____

_____

_____

_____

_____

_____

_____

Step 5: **Receive God's Perspective** (Fill Up).

Ask the Lord to fill your spirit with His words.

Write down what you hear Him say.

Step 6: **Re-Read and Review** (Pay Attention).

    What stands out to you?

    List key/highlighted parts of God's message to you.

_____

_____

_____

_____

_____

_____

_____

Step 7: **Renew Your Mind** (Find the Truth).

    What specific truth does God want you to
    incorporate into your life today?

_____

_____

_____

_____

_____

_____

_____

Step 8: **Remove and Replace** (Recognize - and Make - the Beautiful Exchange). What exchange does Jesus offer you?

       Today I Release ⟶

       and replace it with ⟶

Step 9: **Respond** (Take Action).

What step of faith do you sense God inviting you to take?

_____

_____

_____

Step 10: **Explore the Resistance** (Discern any Hesitation or Pushback).

What feelings come up for you when you receive an invitation to walk in bold, active faith? Where/how do you feel hesitation or pushback in your spirit?

_____

_____

_____

_____

Step 11: **Reach Out** (Seek Confirmation).

What counsel would help you to move forward?

_____

_____

_____

_____

Step 12: **Reflect** (Testify)!

What would you like to say to the Lord to close your journaling time? Write a word back to God in response to what you received today.

_____

_____

_____

_____

Chronicle your beautiful exchange in the back of the book.

Today's Date   Check in word, how are you feeling right now?

_____   _____

Step 1: Get Rooted in Scripture (Anchor).

    Take a moment to marinate in the following passage.

> "The Spirit is the one who gives
> life. The flesh doesn't help at all.
> The words that I have spoken to
> you are spirit and are life."
>
> **— John 6:63**

Step 2: Record the Key Message (Notice).

    What Kingdom truth is God highlighting to you in this passage?

_____

_____

_____

_____

_____

Step 3: Recognize God's Goodness (Gratitude).

    List three things you are grateful for today.

_____

_____

_____

_____

_____

Step 4: **Release and Request** (Pour Out).

Pour out your honest questions and concerns to the Lord. What do you want to address with him?

Step 5: **Receive God's Perspective** (Fill Up).

Ask the Lord to fill your spirit with His words.
Write down what you hear Him say.

Step 6: **Re-Read and Review** (Pay Attention).
       What stands out to you?
       List key/highlighted parts of God's message to you.

_____

_____

_____

_____

_____

_____

_____

Step 7: **Renew Your Mind** (Find the Truth).
       What specific truth does God want you to
       incorporate into your life today?

_____

_____

_____

_____

_____

_____

Step 8: **Remove and Replace** (Recognize - and Make - the Beautiful Exchange). What exchange does Jesus offer you?

Today I Release $\longrightarrow$

and replace it with $\longrightarrow$

Step 9: **Respond** (Take Action).

What step of faith do you sense God inviting you to take?

Step 10: **Explore the Resistance** (Discern any Hesitation or Pushback).

What feelings come up for you when you receive an invitation to walk in bold, active faith? Where/how do you feel hesitation or pushback in your spirit?

Step 11: **Reach Out** (Seek Confirmation).

What counsel would help you to move forward?

Step 12: **Reflect** (Testify)!

What would you like to say to the Lord to close your journaling time? Write a word back to God in response to what you received today.

Chronicle your beautiful exchange in the back of the book.

Today's Date   Check in word, how are you feeling right now?

Step 1: **Get Rooted in Scripture** (Anchor).

Take a moment to marinate in the following passage.

"For we are his workmanship,
created in Christ Jesus for good
works, which God prepared
ahead of time for us to do."

— **Ephesians 2:10**

Step 2: **Record the Key Message** (Notice).

What Kingdom truth is God highlighting to you in this passage?

Step 3: **Recognize God's Goodness** (Gratitude).

List three things you are grateful for today.

Step 4: **Release and Request** (Pour Out).

  Pour out your honest questions and concerns to the Lord.
  What do you want to address with him?

Step 5: **Receive God's Perspective** (Fill Up).

Ask the Lord to fill your spirit with His words.

Write down what you hear Him say.

Step 6: **Re-Read and Review** (Pay Attention).
What stands out to you?
List key/highlighted parts of God's message to you.

_____

_____

_____

_____

_____

_____

_____

Step 7: **Renew Your Mind** (Find the Truth).
What specific truth does God want you to
incorporate into your life today?

_____

_____

_____

_____

_____

_____

Step 8: **Remove and Replace** (Recognize - and Make - the Beautiful
Exchange). What exchange does Jesus offer you?

Today I Release $\longrightarrow$

and replace it with $\longrightarrow$

Step 9: **Respond** (Take Action).

What step of faith do you sense God inviting you to take?

_____

_____

_____

Step 10: **Explore the Resistance** (Discern any Hesitation or Pushback).

What feelings come up for you when you receive an invitation to walk in bold, active faith? Where/how do you feel hesitation or pushback in your spirit?

_____

_____

_____

Step 11: **Reach Out** (Seek Confirmation).

What counsel would help you to move forward?

_____

_____

_____

Step 12: **Reflect** (Testify)!

What would you like to say to the Lord to close your journaling time? Write a word back to God in response to what you received today.

_____

_____

_____

Chronicle your beautiful exchange in the back of the book.

Today's Date   Check in word, how are you feeling right now?

_____   _____

Step 1: Get Rooted in Scripture (Anchor).
Take a moment to marinate in the following passage.

"For the word of God is living and effective
and sharper than any double-edged sword,
penetrating as far as the separation of soul
and spirit, joints and marrow. It is able to
judge the thoughts and intentions of the heart."

— Hebrews 4:12

Step 2: Record the Key Message (Notice).
What Kingdom truth is God highlighting to you in this passage?

_____

_____

_____

_____

_____

Step 3: Recognize God's Goodness (Gratitude).
List three things you are grateful for today.

_____

_____

_____

_____

_____

Step 4: **Release and Request** (Pour Out).

Pour out your honest questions and concerns to the Lord.
What do you want to address with him?

Step 5: **Receive God's Perspective** (Fill Up).

Ask the Lord to fill your spirit with His words.

Write down what you hear Him say.

Step 6: **Re-Read and Review** (Pay Attention).
What stands out to you?
List key/highlighted parts of God's message to you.

_____

_____

_____

_____

_____

_____

_____

Step 7: **Renew Your Mind** (Find the Truth).
What specific truth does God want you to
incorporate into your life today?

_____

_____

_____

_____

_____

_____

Step 8: **Remove and Replace** (Recognize - and Make - the Beautiful
Exchange). What exchange does Jesus offer you?

Today I Release $\longrightarrow$

and replace it with $\longrightarrow$

Step 9: **Respond** (Take Action).

What step of faith do you sense God inviting you to take?

_____

_____

_____

Step 10: **Explore the Resistance** (Discern any Hesitation or Pushback).

What feelings come up for you when you receive an invitation
to walk in bold, active faith? Where/how do you feel hesitation
or pushback in your spirit?

_____

_____

_____

Step 11: **Reach Out** (Seek Confirmation).

What counsel would help you to move forward?

_____

_____

_____

Step 12: **Reflect** (Testify)!

What would you like to say to the Lord to close your
journaling time? Write a word back to God in response
to what you received today.

_____

_____

_____

Chronicle your beautiful exchange in the back of the book.

Beautiful
Exchange

Record: Chronicle the Beautiful Exchange!

What are the gifts you received from Jesus in the pages of this book? It will be amazing to read this list over time and see just how faithful He is . . .

Date: _____ I release _____, and replace with _____.

Date: _____ I release _____, and replace with _____.

Date: _____ I release _____, and replace with _____.

Date: _____ I release _____, and replace with _____.

Date: _____ I release _____, and replace with _____.

Date: _____ I release _____, and replace with _____.

Date: _____ I release _____, and replace with _____.

Date: _____ I release _____, and replace with _____.

Date: _____ I release _____, and replace with _____.

Date: _____ I release _____, and replace with _____.

Date: _____ I release _____, and replace with _____.

Date: _____ I release _____, and replace with _____.

Date: _____ I release _____, and replace with _____.

Date: _____ I release _____, and replace with _____.

Date: _____ I release _____, and replace with _____.

Date: _____ I release _____, and replace with _____.

Date: _____ I release _____, and replace with _____.

Date: _____ I release _____, and replace with _____.

Date: _____ I release _____, and replace with _____.

Date: _____ I release _____, and replace with _____.

Date: _____ I release _____, and replace with _____.

Date: _____ I release _____, and replace with _____.

Date: _____ I release _____, and replace with _____.

Date: _____ I release _____, and replace with _____.

Date: _____ I release _____, and replace with _____.

Date: _____ I release _____, and replace with _____.

Date: _____ I release _____, and replace with _____.

Date: _____ I release _____, and replace with _____.

Date: _____ I release _____, and replace with _____.

Date: _____ I release _____, and replace with _____.

About the Author

Megan Nilsen has experienced a varied work life doing everything from retail (which she hated) to school counseling (which she loved). Working as a Kingdom Life Coach, she empowers people of all ages to listen to the voice of God and take aligned action in a world of possibilities. Her previous work includes the books *Untangled Faith: How Honest Conversations with God Lead to Deeper Connections, Clarity, and Peace*, and *A Beautiful Exchange: Responding to God's Invitation for More*. Get to know her and join the honest, untangling conversations of life and faith at *The Kingdom Life Coaching Podcast* wherever you listen to podcasts! She lives in Colorado. Megan and her husband have four children at different launching stages as we speak.

If you have been blessed by this journal, please share the message with others by posting on social media using #abeautifulexchangejournal

Website: www.meganbnilsen.com

Podcast: The Kingdom Life Coaching Podcast

 Megan Bradley Nilsen

 @megan_nilsen

Other Titles
by Megan Nilsen

A Beautiful Exchange

Megan's journey leads her to discover the Kingdom of God and live her true identity, demonstrating that God's highest calling is the same for everyone.

Untangled Faith

How Honest Conversations with God Lead to Deeper Connections, Clarity, and Peace

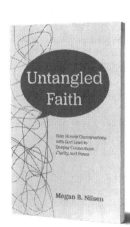